The Decorated Frame

The Decorated Frame

45 PICTURE-PERFECT PROJECTS

Joe Rhatigan

LARK BOOKS

A Division of Sterling Publishing Co., Inc.
New York

Art Director: DANA IRWIN

Assistant Art Director: HANNES CHAREN

Cover Design: BARBARA ZARETSKY

Photography: SANDRA STAMBAUGH

Illustrations: ORRIN LUNDGREN

Library of Congress Cataloging-in-Publication Data Available

10 9 8 7 6 5 4 3 2 1

First Edition

Published by Lark Books, a division of
Sterling Publishing Co., Inc.
387 Park Avenue South, New York, N.Y. 10016

© 2002, Lark Books

Distributed in Canada by Sterling Publishing,
c/o Canadian Manda Group, One Atlantic Ave., Suite 105
Toronto, Ontario, Canada M6K 3E7

Distributed in the U.K. by:
Guild of Master Craftsman Publications Ltd.
Castle Place, 166 High Street Lewes East Sussex, England BN7 1XU
Tel: (+ 44) 1273 477374 Fax: (+ 44) 1273 478606
Email: pubs@thegmcgroup.com, Web: www.gmcpublications.com

Distributed in Australia by Capricorn Link (Australia) Pty Ltd., P.O. Box
704, Windsor, NSW 2756 Australia

If you have questions or comments about this book, please contact:
Lark Books
67 Broadway
Asheville, NC 28801
(828) 253-0467

Printed in Hong Kong

ISBN 1-57990-339-8

CONTENTS

Perhaps we, as humans, have something deep in our brains that instinctively wants to create boundaries to contain and protect the beauty we seek in the world around us. Or, maybe picture frames exist to bestow importance on the images they hold, and in the process, become works of art themselves. Whatever the reasons, frames are an important, if not essential, part of home decor.

These days you can purchase picture frames just about anywhere: large grocery stores, discount outlet stores, and even home improvement centers. There are times when you can find exactly what you're looking for in one of these locations, but often, finding the "perfect frame" can be frustrating. If you want something that's original and distinctive and expresses your own personality and style, then you'll have to take matters into your own creative hands. That's where this book comes in.

There are books out there that go into great detail about frame making, matting, glass cutting, and other useful information when you're interested in creating frames from scratch. This book, however, is unique in that it focuses solely on decorating existing frames—whether it's a paint-encrusted cast-off you found at a yard sale or an unfinished frame from the craft store. With the projects in this book, you'll be inspired to personalize a wide variety of purchased frames with paint, fabric, wire, beads, paper, costume jewelry, pencils, doorknobs, flowers, fripperies, and more. Each project, whether it has that restrained elegant look you've been searching for or that special far-out, break-every-framing-rule-in-the-book look, is accessible, uncomplicated, and, most of all, fun.

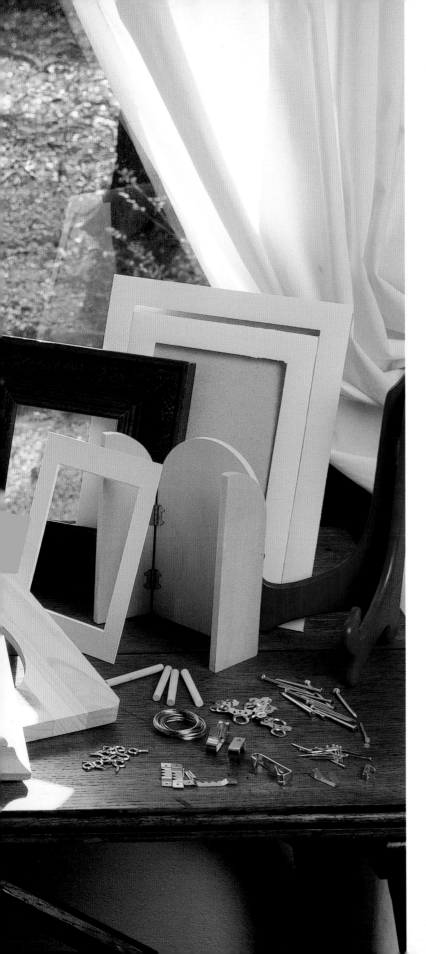

There are several kinds of frames you might use for the projects in this book, and there are just as many ways of getting them. You can buy unfinished frames from a craft store. These plain, wooden frames provide a great surface for paint and other techniques. In most cases, you'll have to buy the glass and backing separately. There are also those tired-looking frames you have kicking around the house that you just can't stand to look at anymore. And yard sales and attics are great places to find old frames that simply need some creativity on your part in order for them to shine.

No matter where your frames are coming from, you won't need any special knowledge to begin the projects in this book. However, the following lists will familiarize you with some simple techniques and reminders to get you started.

Many craft stores have extensive framing sections that include several varieties of unfinished and finished frames, mats, glazes, and hanging materials. The bigger craft stores may also be able to cut glass for you.

Frame Preparation and Painting Tips

Many of the frames in this book call for you to do some initial preparation and/or painting. Here are some overall tips if you feel a little shaky when it comes to painting.

1 Acrylic craft paints are the easiest paints to use when decorating a wooden frame. There are many brands available, as well as hundreds of colors. Acrylic paints dry quickly and clean easily with water and soap. Check out the acrylic spray paints for an even simpler painting experience.

2 Before you start painting or using spray glues, create adequate ventilation, and completely cover your work surface with newspaper.

3 Elevate the frame on a piece of scrap wood or jar before applying paint.

4 If you notice the wood grain showing through a brand new coat of paint after it's dried, lightly sand the frame down with 400-grit sandpaper and apply another coat. Re-coat your painted frame until you're happy with the results.

5 Don't forget to paint the inside and outside edges of your frame. In most cases, you'll also want to paint the back of the frame.

6 If you're preparing a painted wooden frame, and wish to strip it first, begin by sanding it with surface-removal sandpaper. Remove all sanding dust with a slightly damp cloth. Then sand the frame as smooth as possible, first using 200-grit, and then the 400-grit sandpapers. Finally, apply two light coats of primer to the frame.

7 If using an old, slightly beat-up frame, fill any indentations, holes, or slight imperfections in the wood with wood putty, smoothing it out with your finger. After the putty dries (usually just a few minutes for a light application), sand the frame with 200-grit sandpaper. Finish sanding with 400-grit sandpaper.

8 If using an unfinished frame, sand the frame as smooth as possible, first using 200-grit, and then 400-grit sandpapers. Remove all sanding dust with a slightly damp cloth. Apply a primer, if desired.

9 There are a variety of finishes you can apply to your painted frame. When you don't wish to change the painted appearance, simply use matte acrylic spray sealer. For more sheen, use a satin or gloss finish.

10 When painting glass, remember that glass is nonporous, so you need to clean the surface thoroughly to remove grease, fingerprints, and smudges, or the paint may not adhere properly. Clean with a mild detergent and water or with glass cleaner (vinegar mixed with water works well). If the paint manufacturer's instructions recommend applying surface conditioner after cleaning the glass, make sure to take this extra step. Also read manufacturer's instructions regarding baking the glass after painting. Finally, practice on junk glass before starting on your frame.

DON'T FORGET TO...

1 Consider the photograph, print, artwork, etc., before creating the frame. Some may look better with an elegant frame, while others demand something silly. You can always alter the projects to fit more appropriately with the photographs you're using.

2 Consider where the frame will hang or stand. Will it clash with the drapes or complement the rug? Alter paint colors and fabrics used accordingly.

3 Practice any unfamiliar techniques on a piece of scrap paper, wood, or glass before working on the frame.

4 Remove the backing, insides, and glass before working on a frame.

5 Consider that the inside dimensions of your frame will be different if you wrap the frame with a material, such as metal or fabric, and you may have to have the glass recut to make it fit back into the frame.

6 Paint or otherwise decorate the back of your frame if it's going to be standing on a tabletop.

7 Use all materials according to manufacturer's instructions.

Asian Infusion

DESIGNER: ALLISON SMITH

A bamboo stamp, a couple of large Chinese coins, and two tassels are all you need to spice up a store-bought black frame and evoke the exotic flavor of the Far East.

WHAT YOU NEED

Wooden frame, any size

Black acrylic spray paint

Gold ink pad

Bamboo stamp

Spray acrylic sealer, gloss finish

2 large Chinese coins with hole in center★

Small gold tassels

Hot glue gun with glue sticks

★Available wherever beading supplies are sold

WHAT YOU DO

1 Find a black frame, or paint a wooden frame with one or two coats of the black acrylic spray paint. Let it dry.

2 Load the bamboo stamp with gold ink. Carefully stamp across the long sides of the frame. Match the ends of the stamp so that they're even and touching. The goal is to make the finished stamp look like one stalk of bamboo. If you make a mistake, wipe it off immediately with water. Then, dry it off and try it again.

3 Spray the frame with several coats of the sealer.

4 Attach the tassels to the backs of the coins with a dot of hot glue, and immediately press the coins onto the short sides of the frames.

Create a fabulous, contemporary frame by weaving complementary or contrasting colors of ribbons. Use organza ribbon if you wish to create a sheer effect.

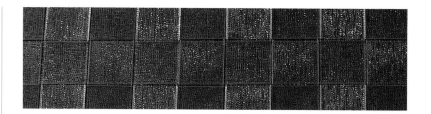

Ribbon Weave

DESIGNER: ALLISON SMITH

WHAT YOU DO

1 Measure the width and height of the frame. Add 2 inches (5.1 cm) to the height, and cut enough ribbon to line up edge to edge across the top of the frame. For example, if the frame is 5 inches (12.7 cm) wide and your ribbon is ½ inch (1.3 cm) wide, you'll need to cut 10 ribbons. Remember that the ribbons in the center of the frame only need to be half as long.

2 Cut the ribbons that will be woven horizontally the same way.

3 Use hot glue to attach the ends of the ribbons to the top backside of the frame. Alternate colors as you go along, and keep the edges of the ribbon as close together as you can without overlapping.

4 Starting at the top of the frame, attach the first horizontal ribbon to the top left side of the frame. (Remember to attach the ribbon to the back of the frame.) In other words, this ribbon should be at the very top left corner of the frame.

5 Weave the ribbon in and out of the ribbons hanging down from the top, and secure it on the back of the right side of the frame with hot glue.

6 Continue weaving with alternating ribbons. Be sure to keep the edges straight and close together. As you continue weaving, gently pull the vertical ribbons to keep them straight and flat.

7 When weaving the short side edges of the frame, simply weave to the center opening, secure the ribbon on the back inside center of the frame with hot glue, and trim the ribbon. Secure the remaining ribbon on the opposite edge with hot glue, and continue weaving. Attach the end of the ribbon on the right side of the frame with hot glue.

8 To conceal the back of the frame, trace the frame onto the piece of posterboard. Cut out the shape, and trim the edges so they don't stick out around the edges of the frame. Spray with adhesive, and cover with fabric. Wrap the edges around the posterboard to make a clean edge. Attach to the back of the frame with hot glue in order to conceal the raw edges of the ribbon.

WHAT YOU NEED

Flat wooden frame, any size (the wider the borders, the better)

Ruler

Two different colors of ribbon

Scissors

Hot glue gun and glue sticks

Posterboard

12 x 12-inch (30.5 x 30.5 cm) scrap of fabric in a coordinating color

Spray adhesive

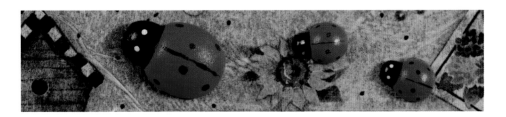

Gardener's Delight

DESIGNER: ALLISON SMITH

WHAT YOU DO

1 Paint the frame with one or two coats of green acrylic spray paint. Let it dry.

2 Paint the frame with a heavy coat of decoupage medium.

3 Lay a sheet of the gardening theme tissue paper down on a flat surface with the right side facing down. Position the frame on top of the tissue paper. Flip the frame and paper over and gently smooth the paper out.

4 Secure any loose edges with a drop of the decoupage medium. Wrap the paper around the frame, snipping the paper with scissors and folding the paper to make a neat fit (like wrapping a present). Let the frame dry.

5 Since the tissue paper is thin, you don't really need to go over the covered frame with another coat of decoupage medium. However, if you're using wrapping paper or some other thicker paper, definitely slap on a coat of medium over the frame. If you want to further protect the frame, you could also spray it with the clear acrylic sealer.

6 Attach the rake and shovel to the sides of the frame with hot glue.

7 Glue the ladybugs to the top and bottom of the frame and wherever else you think they might be happy.

The wooden ladybugs that embellish this frame are as welcome as their real counterparts are in the garden. This is the perfect gardener's gift.

WHAT YOU NEED

Wooden frame, any size

Green acrylic spray paint

Decoupage medium

Small sponge brush

Garden theme tissue paper

Scissors

Spray acrylic sealer of your choice (optional)

4-inch (10.2 cm) shovel and rake★

Hot glue gun and glue sticks

Small- and medium-sized wooden ladybugs★

★Available from craft suppliers

A simple sponged-paint treatment gives the illusion of flora as seen in a sunlight-dappled forest. To get this delicate look, use young or miniature specialty ferns.

Forest Foliage

DESIGNER: SUZANNE NICAUD

WHAT YOU NEED

Wooden frame, any size

Spray paint primer

Acrylic craft paints in pale yellow, spring green, deep olive green, and a reddish brown

Muffin tin-style plastic paint palette

1 small sea wool sponge (slightly rough texture)

1 small sea silk sponge (fine-grained texture)

Freshly cut fern fronds

Yellow acrylic spray paint

Paper towel

Metallic wax, aged gold (optional)★

Small wooden skewer and cotton balls (optional)

Spray acrylic sealer of your choice

★Available from craft suppliers

WHAT YOU DO

1 Paint the frame with one or two coats of the primer. Let it dry.

2 Pour a small amount of each of the acrylic paints into the muffin-style palette.

3 Thoroughly wet the sponges, then squeeze them very dry before using. If they're new, squeeze mild sudsy water through them first, then rinse them before starting. Use the rough-textured sponge to apply random areas of each of the four paint colors to the frame, turning the sponge for each new color, in order to keep the colors clean. Cover all sides of the frame, and don't forget the inside and outside edges. Be sure not to let the paint dry in the sponges.

4 Find an area in the fine-grained sponge with the least amount of texture in it. Before the paint is dry, dip this part of the sponge into one of the colors, and apply the color randomly over the previous coat. To get a soft, dappled effect, use very firm pressure. Rinse the sponge between colors so that you can use the same fine-grained area of the sponge for each of the colors. Let the paint dry.

5 Lay a fern frond down on the frame, and hold it in place. With the yellow acrylic spray paint, spray a very light coat over the fern to create its outline on the painted frame, but don't spray so heavily that the areas surrounding the fern are-blocked by an opaque coat of the spray paint. Move the frond around, or use a fresh one for each repeat of the spray technique.

6 While the spray paint is still wet, work the darker craft paint colors back over the spray-painted areas that surround the fern's outlines. Use a very dry sponging technique and very little paint, blotting the sponge on a paper towel first. Carefully fill in any areas that appear too light, without obliterating the fern's outline. Let the paint dry.

7 If your frame has a fillet surrounding the frame's opening, use your finger to apply and smooth small amounts of the metallic wax onto the fillet. Wrap a small amount of cotton, pulled from a cotton ball, onto the pointed tip of the skewer. Use this to work the metallic wax into the corners of the fillet.

8 Spray the frame lightly with one or two coats of the sealer.

18

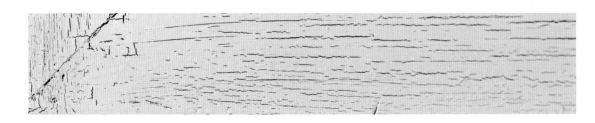

Snap Crackle

DESIGNER: PAULA HEYES

This instant aging technique is achieved with white craft glue instead of crackle medium. The effect is wonderful, and you actually have more flexibility and time to achieve the look you want.

WHAT YOU DO

1 Paint the frame a dark color that will stand out when the top coat "cracks." Let it dry.

2 Paint the front and inside and outside edges of the frame with the white glue. The glue will be thick, but don't dilute it. Make sure the coat is even. Allow the glue to dry completely.

3 Paint the top coat with the white paint. As you paint, consider these points: the cracks will run in the direction you paint; the thicker the paint, the bigger the cracks; and unlike other crackle mediums, in which you can only paint one stroke, you actually have a longer working time and can go back over an area until you have the coverage you want.

4 Let the frame dry overnight. Finish the frame with a coat or two of the acrylic sealer.

WHAT YOU NEED

Wooden frame, any size

Acrylic paint in your choice of color

Paintbrushes

White craft glue

White paint (or color of your choice)

Spray acrylic sealer of your choice

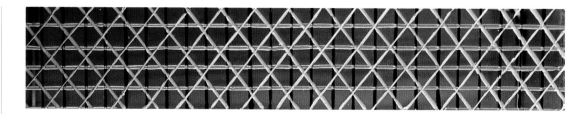

Faux Metallic

DESIGNER: DIANA LIGHT

A woven pattern of gold, silver, copper, and black paints provides a textured backdrop for a favorite photo.

WHAT YOU NEED

Double glass frame or document frame that holds paper between pieces of clear glass

Grid design template (see page 94)

Spray glass cleaner

Photo

Scissors

Glass liner paint in gold, silver, copper, and black★

★These paints come in tubes and bottles equipped with tips for squeezing the paint into consistent lines. Moving slowly with the liner tip renders a wider line; moving quickly thins it.

WHAT YOU DO

1 Enlarge the template to a size that fits your frame. (You can trim the edges if needed, since the template is an overall pattern.) Cut the template to the size of the frame if necessary.

2 Remove the two pieces of glass, and clean them with the glass cleaner.

3 Place the template faceup between the two pieces of glass, and place them back in the frame so the lines show through the front piece of glass. Place the photo you plan on using in the frame on top of the template, and center it between the two pieces of glass.

4 Practice using the black outliner on a sheet of paper or a glass jar from your recycling bin to get a feel for using the liners. To begin making a line, squeeze the paint out of the tip, and touch the tip to the glass. When you reach the end of the line, lift the tip off the glass about ¼ inch (6 mm) while still squeezing, allowing the line to fall to the surface.

5 Begin drawing lines of paint on the glass by laying a black rectangular shape that's the size of your photo. Follow the lines of the grid to place the line.

6 Next, draw in a series of black vertical lines in the frame's border by following the grid. Allow the paint to dry before proceeding.

7 On top of the black lines, layer gold lines in a diagonal pattern by following the grid.

8 After you've allowed the gold lines to dry, lay the copper lines on top in a horizontal pattern by following the grid.

9 After the copper lines have dried, lay a series of silver lines on top of all the lines to create the final woven look.

10 Follow the paint manufacturer's instructions for either drying or baking the paint.

Salvage Style

DESIGNER: JEAN MOORE

Decorating a large frame with salvaged hardware is a classy way of reusing old architectural elements that need a new home. If you don't have any hardware kicking around the house, visit your local architectural salvage store or check online.

WHAT YOU NEED

Wooden frame, any size

Dark wood stain

Paintbrush

4 or more antique hardware elements, such as keyholes, knobs, skeleton keys, and drawer pulls

Drill, with assorted bits

Screws to fit holes in hardware elements

Screwdriver

Nuts (for drawer pulls)

WHAT YOU DO

1 When deciding on how to proceed with this project, make sure you either choose a frame size according to the size of the hardware you have on hand, or choose the hardware according to the size of the frame you want to use. In other words, a large doorknob on a small frame may look funny.

2 Find a dark-stained wooden frame, or stain a wooden frame. Let it dry.

3 Lay the frame on your work surface, and place the various pieces of hardware you've collected on the frame until you're pleased with the arrangement.

4 Drill pilot holes through the existing holes in the hardware.

5 Screw the hardware pieces into place.

6 If you're using a drawer pull, drill a hole into the frame to hold the stem of the pull in place. Then secure the stem with a nut on the backside of the frame.

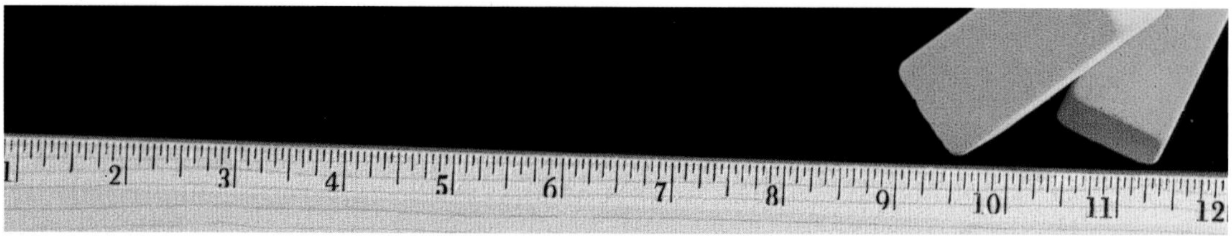

School Daze

DESIGNER: ALLISON SMITH

There's no denying the appeal of this charming school-themed frame. Keep a piece of chalk in the well, and draw temporary designs on the frame to fit any mood.

WHAT YOU NEED

10 x 12-inch (25.4 x 30.5 cm) flat wooden frame with wide borders*

Black chalkboard spray paint

1 x 2 x 12-inch (2.5 x 5.1 x 30.5 cm) poplar board

Hot glue gun with glue sticks

12-inch (30.5 cm) wooden ruler

2 pink erasers

4 pencils

Pencil sharpener

*If you want to use a smaller frame, first find a wooden ruler that's the same size as the width of the frame you wish to use.

WHAT YOU DO

1 Spray the frame (front and back) with several coats of the black chalkboard paint. Let the frame dry.

2 Run a line of hot glue along the bottom edge of the frame, and attach the poplar board so that it's flush across the back of the frame and there's a 1-inch (2.5 cm) (approximately) overhang across the front.

3 Run a line of hot glue across the front of the board, and attach the wooden ruler to the front, creating the chalk well.

4 Glue the erasers to a bottom corner of the frame.

5 Sharpen the pencils until they're the right lengths to create a border around the inside edge of the frame. Arrange and glue the pencils around the inside edge.

Sunny Citrus

DESIGNER: MARTHE LE VAN

Leave a good impression with this enjoyable stamping method. The designer remembers using this technique as a child to decorate the family's bathroom.

WHAT YOU DO

1 Paint the frame with the lime green paint. Let it dry.

2 Place one orange on top of the kitchen cutting board. Use the kitchen knife to cut the orange in half, horizontally slicing through the middle of the fruit.

3 Use the paring knife to remove the flesh from one half of the orange, while leaving the raised divisions intact. Once the flesh is removed from all sections, drain the remaining juice from the orange half onto a paper towel. Repeat with the other half, then allow the orange halves to air-dry for about 30 minutes.

4 While the orange dries, repeat steps 2 and 3 with two lemons.

5 Mix the orange acrylic paint, pour some onto the flat plastic lid, and evenly spread it into a circle larger than the orange. Lightly press the orange half into the paint, then stamp it onto a piece of scrap paper. If your stamp is too heavy, press the fruit on the paper again without applying additional paint. Use the fine-tip paintbrush to fill in any orange skin sections that aren't taking paint. Repeat this testing process until you're happy with the results.

6 Use the technique in step 5 to stamp the oranges onto your painted frame. Leave plenty of room between the oranges to accommodate the later addition of lemons. Vary the placement of the orange stamps on your frame, and even let a few trail off the edges. If your stamp loses its definition, use another orange half. Let the paint dry.

7 Wash off the plastic lid, and repeat steps 5 and 6 using the yellow paint and one lemon half. Let some of the lemon stamps partially overlap the orange stamps. Let the yellow paint dry.

8 Wash off the plastic lid again, and repeat steps 5 and 6, this time with the second lemon half and the tangerine paint. If desired, spray the frame lightly with one or two coats of the sealer.

WHAT YOU NEED

Wooden frame, any size

Acrylic craft paints in lime green, lemon yellow, orange, and tangerine

Paintbrush

2 firm and well-shaped oranges★

Kitchen cutting board

Kitchen knife

Paring knife

Paper towels

2 or 3 firm and well-shaped lemons★

Flat plastic lid

Fine-tip paintbrush

Spray acrylic sealer of your choice (optional)

★You may not need to use all the pieces of fruit; however, it's a good idea to have extras available.

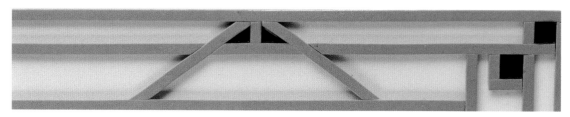

Architect's Dream

DESIGNER: DIANA LIGHT

Bold borders and angles give this sleek frame architectural appeal. Simulated lead lines and stained glass paint are all it takes to complete this singular frame.

WHAT YOU NEED

Glass clip frame, any size

Glass cleaner

Paper towels, or a lint-free cloth

Photocopy of template (see page 94), sized to fit your frame

Transparent tape

Self-adhesive simulated lead lines, ⅛ inch (3 mm) wide, in silver

Craft knife

Water-based, air-drying, simulated stained glass paint, in green

Plastic applicator bottle

Small applicator tip

Straight pin

WHAT YOU DO

1 Clean both sides of the frame glass with glass cleaner and a paper towel.

2 Place the photocopied template on your work surface with the design facing up. Place the glass on top of the template, and make sure that the design is centered and level. Using pieces of transparent tape, secure the template to the glass.

3 Peel one self-adhesive lead line off the backing paper. Press the lead line onto the glass following the design template. Use the craft knife to cut the lead line to the right length.

4 Continue to apply the lead lines until the design is complete. Where two or more lines intersect, don't overlap the lead lines. Instead, carefully cut the lines to join where they meet.

5 Mix the green simulated stained glass paint. Pour a small amount of the paint into the plastic applicator bottle. Attach the small applicator tip to the top of the bottle, and make a tight seal.

6 Fill in the small squares and triangles with the green stained glass paint. Use the straight pin to pop any air bubbles that appear in the paint. Allow the paint to dry.

Rad Plaid

DESIGNER: SUZANNE NICAUD

Use the suggested colors or experiment with others for this fresh, funky, and modern plaid.

WHAT YOU NEED

Wooden frame with flat surface, any size

Spray acrylic paints in yellow, green, and purple

Roll of 1-inch-wide (2.5 cm) masking tape

Roll of ¼-inch-wide (6 mm) masking tape★

Spray acrylic sealer of your choice

★You can find ¼-inch-wide (6 mm) tape where quilters' supplies are sold.

WHAT YOU DO

1 Paint the frame with one or two coats of yellow acrylic spray paint. Let it dry.

2 Mask off some vertical and horizontal stripes of varying widths with the 1-inch (2.5 cm) tape. Have fun with the design. Sure, plan it out a bit, but also let a little serendipity into the design.

3 Then, respray the frame with the purple paint. Don't forget the edges!

4 Repeat steps 2 and 3, using the ¼-inch (6 mm) tape and the green paint.

5 Wait until the green paint is dry, and carefully remove all the tape. Finish the frame with a coat or two of the acrylic sealer.

No-Toil Foil
DESIGNER: ALLISON SMITH

Simulated metallic leaf creates an instant timeless effect that'll look perfect in almost any room. The foil leaf is very thin and delicate, and any slight imperfections that appear after applying it only add to the appeal.

WHAT YOU DO

1 Find a dark-colored frame, or paint a wooden frame with one or two coats of the brownish-red acrylic spray paint. Let it dry.

2 Measure the frame's width and height. Divide the measurements in half to find the center point of each. Mark these lines with a very straight pencil line.

3 Use the masking tape and paper to section off two opposite corners of the frame.

4 Place the frame on a sheet of newspaper. Spray the two exposed corners with the foil leaf adhesive. Make sure to coat the edges.

5 Simulated leaf foil usually comes sandwiched between pages in a book. The foil is really thin and has a tendency to go where you don't want it to go. However, instead of using your fingers to pick up the foil, simply place a piece of wax paper on top of the foil. The wax paper has enough static cling to pick up the foil without much fuss.

6 Place the wax paper with the leaf clinging to it onto a section of the frame with the adhesive on it. Try not to stick the wax paper to the frame, and gently peel away the wax paper, leaving only the foil behind.

7 Start with bigger pieces of foil, and then fill in spaces with smaller pieces. Use the dry paintbrush to move the foil around and make sure it's securely attached. Use the tip of the brush to pick up little pieces to dab on empty spots.

8 Rub the paper towel or soft cloth over the surface. This burnishes the leaf and gives it a nice sheen, while also removing any excess leaf.

9 To repeat the process with the other two sections, carefully place a white sheet of paper over the gold sections, and tape it on the backside of the frame. If you place tape on the finished gold leaf, it'll pull the leaf off when you remove the tape.

10 Spray the frame with the adhesive, and apply the silver leaf as you did before.

11 Turn the frame over and spray the entire back of the frame with adhesive. Apply the silver leaf.

WHAT YOU NEED

Wooden frame, any size

Acrylic spray paint in any brownish-red color

Ruler

Masking tape

Plain white paper

Newspaper

Foil spray adhesive

Simulated gold and silver foil leaf

Wax paper

Small paintbrush

Paper towels or soft cloth

Floral Fantasy

DESIGNER: DIANA LIGHT

Everything will be comin' up roses (or, in this case, hydrangeas) when you turn an old, beat-up frame into a fanciful flowerbed that'll brighten up any room.

WHAT YOU NEED

Flat wooden frame, any size

Acrylic spray paint in base color of flowers

2 to 3 bunches of fake flowers

Scissors

Hot glue gun and glue sticks

WHAT YOU DO

1 Paint the frame in a complementary color to the flowers.

2 Pull or cut the fake flowers off the stems, and separate them by color. The flowers for this project either had white or purple centers, so they were arranged working from lightest color flowers with white centers in the upper right-hand corner to darker flowers with purple centers in the lower left-hand corner. (The plastic centers of some fake flowers can be pulled out and switched around.)

3 Look and play with your arrangement before you start gluing. Pull off any extra plastic under the flowers.

4 Once you're happy with the arrangement, attach the first flower to the frame with hot glue. Then, start working diagonally in lines across the frame. Plan where you'll place the flowers and how the petals will overlap, so that you won't see the painted surface of the frame. Be sure to check from all angles. Think of the flowers as puzzle pieces. Allow the petals to extend over the edge of the frame on all sides by about ¼ inch (6 mm) and on the inside edges as well.

Jewelry Jitterbug

DESIGNER: SUSAN RIND

Jazz up that boring frame on your bedstand with pieces of costume jewelry embellished with twirls and whirls of wire and beads. This elaborate-looking frame is simple to make, and the results will be unique.

WHAT YOU NEED

Frame of your choice, with at least a 2-inch (5.1 cm) border width

Costume jewelry and other small keepsakes

Wire cutters

Toothpicks

Jewelry glue or epoxy

20-gauge stainless-steel wire

Needle-nose pliers

Round-nose pliers

Assorted faceted and metal beads (4 to 12 mm)

5 to 7 flat-back crystals in assorted colors

WHAT YOU DO

1 Paint the frame, if necessary. Use the wire cutters to remove any unnecessary hardware, such as loops, from the jewelry.

2 Play around with the jewelry until you have a design you like. Use the toothpicks to apply small amounts of the epoxy to the backs of the pieces of jewelry. Avoid excess glue, and apply it sparingly, making sure to cover all flat surfaces that will be in contact with the frame. Depending on the brand of glue you use, you'll have around 10 minutes to play around with the placement before the glue hardens. Allow the glue to dry for 24 hours.

3 Cut off four 20-inch (50.8 cm) lengths of the stainless-steel wire.

4 Loop each wire through the jewelry pieces, and add assorted beads in a random, free-form manner. Play some Miles Davis or John Coltrane to help you improvise. Use the needle-nose pliers to help loop the wires in and out of the jewelry pieces and make small decorative circles.

5 Hide the ends of the wires by tucking them underneath the jewelry pieces or loops of wire.

6 Glue the crystals on the frame where desired.

Transform all those boring glass frames with this etching technique that produces sharp, beautiful images on the glass.

Butterfly Etch

DESIGNER: DIANA LIGHT

WHAT YOU NEED

4 x 6-inch (10.2 x 15.2 cm) metal frame

Glass cleaner

Paper towels

White adhesive shelf paper with peel-off backing

Scissors

Small squeegee

Template (see page 95)

Carbon paper

Tape

Two wallet-sized photos

Ruler

Craft knife with swivel blade

Craft knife

WHAT YOU DO

1 Remove the glass from the frame, and clean it with the glass cleaner.

2 Cut a piece of adhesive shelf paper a little bigger than the glass, peel off the backing, and press it onto the glass. Use the squeegee to remove any air bubbles.

3 Position the template and carbon paper over the glass, and attach them to the glass with tape.

4 Use a pen or pencil to trace the outline of the butterfly and use the ruler to trace the interior picture frame rectangles (use the photgraphs as a guide).

5 Pull off the drawing and carbon paper. Use the swivel blade knife to cut out the butterfly shape. Use the craft knife and ruler to cut the interior rectangles.

6 Pull off the shelf paper butterfly shape, leaving the two rectangles and the shelf paper around the butterfly shape.

7 Lay a piece of discarded shelf paper backing over the glass. Use the squeegee on the backing piece to be sure the shelf paper is making good contact with the glass. (The backing protects the shelf paper from being pulled up by the squeegee by accident.)

8 Take a slightly moistened cotton swab and carefully wipe away any adhesive left on the glass (where you'll be etching).

9 Cut four strips of shelf paper 2 inches (5.1 cm) wide and the length of the glass edges, and lay (stick) them along the edges as a border so no cream will get under the glass by mistake.

10 Follow the instructions on the etch cream bottle. Stir well. Use with good ventilation. Pour a puddle of cream on the border (not on the exposed glass). With the squeegee, quickly pull the cream evenly over the exposed glass. Leave the cream on the glass for the recommended time (ranges from 15 to 30 minutes).

11 If the cream is reusable, squeegee the excess off and back into the bottle, and then rinse and remove all the shelf paper under water. Water makes the etch cream stop working, so it's important to get all of the glass wet as quickly and thoroughly as possible. Once the glass is dry, you're done.

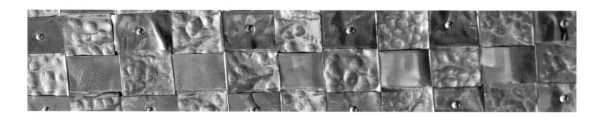

Metal Weave

DESIGNER: TERRY TAYLOR

Weaving with metal strips is not any harder than the construction paper weaving you did in elementary school. Warp and weft are technical words, but you'll have no trouble following the directions.

WHAT YOU NEED

Wooden frame with a broad, flat face

Copper or gold acrylic spray paint

Metric ruler

Calculator

36-gauge metal tooling foils, copper and brass★

Scissors

Awl

½-inch (1.3 cm) brass escutcheon pins

Ball peen hammer (optional)

Craft stick

★Available at craft stores

WHAT YOU DO

1 Paint all sides of the frame with copper or gold paint. Let it dry, then give the frame a second coat, if needed.

2 Measure the width of the frame using the metric ruler. Use the calculator to divide the width of the frame by 1.5 cm, 2 cm, or 2.5 cm. These measurements are good working widths for your warp (vertical weaves). You should get an answer that's close to a whole number such as 8.25 or 14.75. Your answer tells you how many strips you'll need to cut to create the weft (horizontal weave) for your frame. For instance, if your number was 8.25, cut 8 strips and space them further apart. If your answer was 14.75, cut 15 strips and trim a couple of the strips as needed.

3 Before you cut any strips of foil, it's helpful to measure and cut paper equal in width to what you'll use for the warp. Place these strips vertically across the width of the frame. Ideally, you want your warp strips to lie flush with the edges of the frame and the frame's openings. Adjust the placement of the strips as needed, or recalculate using the larger or smaller numbers.

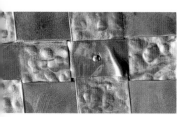

4 Measure the height of the frame as you did in step 2. Follow the directions to determine the number of weft strips you will need. Your weft strips don't have to be the same width as the warp strips!

5 Measure the thickness of your frame. Add three times this measurement to your width and height measurements. Your strips will need to be cut to these measurements. For example, if the height of your frame is 25 cm and the thickness of the frame is 5 cm, cut your strips 40 cm long.

6 Use the ruler and awl to measure and mark the strips you need on the foil. The awl will mark the metal permanently, so use the straight edge of the ruler as a guide for marking.

7 A good rule of thumb is to always check your measurements before you cut. Metal tooling foils are easily cut with scissors. Try to cut the foil strips with a smooth stroke. Watch out for little "stick 'ems" that may pop up as you're cutting the foil. Trim them off with your scissors before you begin to weave the foil strips.

8 If desired, you can texture the metal strips by lightly hammering them with a ball peen hammer.

9 Lay your warp strips on the frame, and position them as desired. Press one end over the bottom edge. Use the awl to pierce a hole in the strip and frame. Tack the strip with an escutcheon pin. Tack the remaining strips so they're all attached to the bottom edge of the frame.

10 Begin weaving with a single strip: over and under the warp strips across the width of the frame. Push the edge of the weft strip flush with the edge of the frame. Pierce and tack both ends in place with escutcheon pins.

11 Anchor the weft strips using escutcheon pins placed at intervals. It's easier to do this as the strips are woven rather than waiting until all the weaving is done.

12 Weave additional strips alternating the over/under pattern with an under/over pattern. This is a plain weave. Other weaving patterns can be used if you wish.

13 The strip at the bottom edge of the frame opening may need to be trimmed to fit flush with the opening. You'll figure this out as you weave the strip. If it isn't flush, remove it and trim the strip to fit.

14 You don't have to weave across the frame opening because you're going to cut these strips later. Simply bring your strip across the warp strips. However, pay attention and continue your weaving pattern as you reach the opposite edge of the opening.

15 When you reach the top edge of the opening and the frame, you may need to trim the strips as you did in step 13.

16 After weaving the last strip, fold the warp strips over the edge of the frame, and tack them in place. Trim the edges of the strips flush with the back of the frame.

17 Use the scissors to cut the warp and weft strips over the frame opening in half. Press the strips against the edges of the opening. Use a craft stick to mold them to the lip of the opening. Then tack the strips in place with escutcheon pins.

Gone Fishin' DESIGNER: ALLISON SMITH

An acrylic magnetic frame adorned with mementos or ornamental miniatures is ideal for showing off your favorite photographs.

WHAT YOU NEED

Clear acrylic magnet frame

Fishing lure with hook dulled or removed

Miniature ornamental fishing rod

Hot glue gun with glue sticks

Pale green vellum paper

Scissors

Fishing photo

WHAT YOU DO

1 Clean the frame with a damp rag. Attach the fishing lure and the fishing rod to the front of the frame with the hot glue.

2 Cut a piece of vellum to act as a background for the photo.

3 Insert the vellum into the frame, and place the photo in the frame at an angle (see project photograph).

Rusty Chic
DESIGNER: JEAN MOORE

For this striking frame, find some old roofing tin, embossed ceiling tiles, rusty bottle caps, old metal jewelry pieces, or any interestingly shaped pieces of flattened rusty metal. (Snoop around parking lots and roadsides.)

WHAT YOU NEED

Sturdy wooden frame

Brown acrylic spray paint

Recycled metal pieces (see above)

Gloves and safety glasses

Tin snips

Nails

Hammer

Industrial-strength adhesive

Bar clamps

WHAT YOU DO

1 Find a brown frame or paint a wooden frame with one or two coats of brown acrylic spray paint. Let it dry.

2 Lay out the various pieces of scrap metal around the frame until you're pleased with the overall composition. You may overlap larger and smaller elements to add texture and visual interest. Wear gloves and safety glasses while handling and cutting the metal pieces.

3 Use the tin snips to cut larger pieces down to size to fit all sides of the frame. When cutting these pieces, leave enough extra metal to overlap the inside and outside edges.

4 Once the pieces are positioned, use nails to attach them to the frame.

5 Use the hammer to bend the tin so that it wraps around the outside edges of the frame. Secure the metal on the outside edges with nails. Don't wrap the metal pieces around the inside edges, as the glass and backing may not fit back into the frame. Simply let the pieces overlap into the opening.

6 After you've attached the larger pieces, it's time to fill in any gaps. Rearrange the smaller elements around the frame, overlapping pieces when necessary. Use the industrial strength adhesive to bond the smaller pieces to the frame. Bar clamps will help to hold the pieces in place while the glue sets.

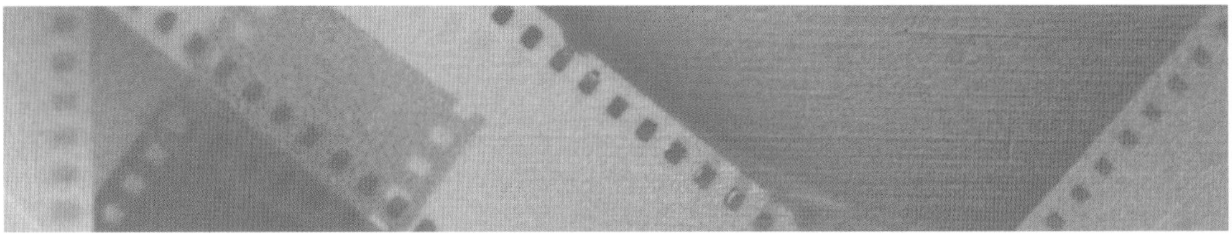

Think Negative

DESIGNER: MARTHE LE VAN

Use this clever, yet uncomplicated, stenciling technique to give an ordinary frame a classy cinematic theme.

WHAT YOU DO

1 Spray paint the frame with the ivory paint. Let it dry. Spray more thin coats of ivory paint onto the frame until you're happy with the results.

2 Position one film negative at an interesting angle across the frame. (Flat negatives work best for this project.) Stick the negative to the frame with a small piece of masking tape. Lightly spray the terra-cotta paint across the film negative, sweeping past its edges and covering its sprocket holes. Let the paint dry. Gently pull the negative off the frame.

3 Repeat step 2 (using the same negative) at two or three more locations on the frame.

4 Tape a new film negative to the frame. (Feel free to adhere it over previously painted areas.) Lightly spray the saffron paint across the film negative, sweeping past its edges and covering its sprocket holes. Let the paint dry. Gently pull the negative off the frame. Repeat this process in several locations.

5 The lightest color spray paint (ivory) can be very useful in completing your design. If you feel that any area is too dark or has become muddy looking, tape down a new negative and spray over it with ivory. The ivory can also provide a new background for further stenciling.

6 Spray the frame with one or two coats of the sealer.

WHAT YOU NEED

Wooden frame, any size

Semigloss spray paints in ivory, terra-cotta, and saffron

3 or more film negative strips

Masking tape

Spray acrylic sealer of your choice

Stellar Stucco

DESIGNER: MARTHE LE VAN

Take some leftover ready-mix joint compound and put it to work creating this delightful frame. Joint compound doesn't smell, dries quickly, and is so easy to work with.

WHAT YOU NEED

Wooden frame, any size

Ready-mix joint compound

1-inch (2.5 cm) plastic putty knife

Plastic fork

Fine-grit sandpaper

Silver acrylic spray paint

WHAT YOU DO

1 Apply a generous amount of ready-mix joint compound onto the frame with the putty knife. Evenly spread the joint compound entirely around the surface of the frame. The joint compound should be approximately ¼ inch (6 mm) thick.

2 Press the plastic fork into the joint compound while it's still wet. When you lift the fork up, little peaks will form in the joint compound. Turn the fork 90° from your first indentation, and press it into the joint compound again, forming a textured grid of peaks.

3 Repeat step 2 to texture the rest of the frame. Work rapidly and evenly, connecting the grids as you go. If any area isn't textured to your liking, simply smooth out the joint compound with your putty knife (adding more if needed), and texture it again. Let the joint compound dry completely.

4 Gently sand off any excess joint compound from the side and interior edges of the frame.

5 Spray paint the frame with the silver paint. Thinly and evenly coat the frame, making sure to hit all the peaks and cover all the frame's visible edges. Let the paint dry. Spray more thin coats of silver paint onto the frame until you achieve a smooth saturation of color.

Woodburning is a fun way to decorate an unfinished frame. With a little practice, you'll be able to create wonderful designs that will complement any print or photograph.

Woodburned Wonder

DESIGNER: SUSAN KIEFFI

WHAT YOU NEED

Unfinished wooden frame, any size

Ruler

Woodburning or branding tool kit, with leaf, script, and all-purpose points

Template (see page 95)

Acrylic sealer of choice (optional)

WHAT YOU DO

1 The woodburned designs on this frame were centered on a 2-inch-wide (5.1 cm) frame border. If the size of your frame differs, change the design locations accordingly.

2 Measure in 1 inch (2.5 cm) from each side of the frame, and very lightly draw a line bisecting the width of each border. These are the center lines you'll use to help place the designs.

3 Either draw your design on a piece of paper cut to the size of the frame, or practice on a piece of scrap wood, until you find a design you like.

4 Screw the leaf design into the tool, and preheat it for approximately five minutes (or follow the manufacturer's directions for preheating). Hold the tool perpendicular to the surface while working, and burn onto one corner of the frame. It takes only two or three seconds to make each mark.

5 Burn a second leaf shape opposite the first, spacing it about ¼ inch (6 mm) away (refer to template on page 95 for more information).

6 Add a third and fourth leaf mark between the first two marks. Repeat this pattern for each of the remaining three corners, and for the centers of the shorter sides of the frame.

7 On the two longer border sides, repeat the leaf patterns, using the pencil marks as the center for each design.

8 Between all the leaf designs, create another pattern using the leaf design, this time overlapping the leaves slightly (refer to template on page 95).

9 Place the tool in its holder, unplug it, and let it cool. Then insert the script point. Preheat the tool. Connect the leaf points with lines burned across the centers. Between the leaves, burn two little curved lines and, using the tip of the script point, make a little mark at the end of each line.

10 Unplug the tool and let it cool. Then insert the all-purpose point. Preheat. Around each of the first leaves created at the corners, centers, etc., burn tiny little marks with the tip of the point. Then, holding the all-purpose point flat against the frame, make lines at the tips of each of these leaves.

11 For the other pattern of leaves, make lines radiating from the point where the leaves connect.

12 Erase the pencil lines, and finish with the acrylic sealer, if you wish.

With this interesting and satisfying technique, you'll produce a look that resembles the intricate series of cracks of delicately aged porcelain.

Napkin Decoupage

DESIGNER: TERRY TAYLOR

WHAT YOU DO

1 Find a white frame, or paint the frame with white paint.

2 Use very sharp scissors to trim motifs from the napkins you have chosen. Trim the motifs closely, but don't worry about being precise. Cut out more motifs than you think you'll need.

3 Arrange the motifs on the frame as desired. Keep in mind that you want part of the motifs to wrap around the sides of the frame when you're arranging them. When you're happy with the arrangement, move the motifs and replicate the arrangement on a flat surface.

4 Apply a thin coat of decoupage medium to one area of the frame. Lift a motif and place it on the coated area. Use the stencil brush to gently pounce the napkin motif to adhere it and prevent air bubbles. If the motif hangs over the side of the frame, give that area a coat of medium, and adhere the medium using the stencil brush. Pounce the brush onto a paper towel to remove excess medium as needed. Repeat these steps until the entire frame has been covered.

5 Brush the applied motifs with a thin coat of medium. Allow the coat to dry.

Then re-coat the frame with one or more coats of medium.

6 Follow the manufacturer's instructions for applying the crackle medium.

7 Paint the frame with an antiquing paint or acrylic paint thinned with a glaze medium, and immediately wipe it off to accent the crackled surface.

WHAT YOU NEED

Wooden frame, any size

White acrylic spray paint

Decorative paper napkins

Scissors

Decoupage medium

Stencil brush

Crackle medium

Dark acrylic paint mixed with glazing medium or acrylic

Experiment with different frames, paints, and hardware pieces until you have the perfect look for this decorative and functional key holder.

Key Holder

DESIGNERS: PAULA AND DALE HEYES

WHAT YOU NEED

Wooden picture frame, any size

Tape measure or ruler

½ x 2-inch (1.3 x 5.1 cm) board (usually sold as molding)

Wood saw

Wood glue

Brads

Tack hammer

¼-inch (6 mm) plywood or beadboard paneling

Paint of your choice

Paintbrush

2 small hinges with screws

Awl

Screwdriver

Kitchen cabinet magnet set

Sandpaper

Small cabinet knob

Drill with assorted bits

Key hooks

WHAT YOU DO

1 Choose the frame for this project according to how big you want your holder to be. Measure the frame for the key box size, and allow for the frame to overlap the box approximately ½ to ¾ inch (1.3 to 1.9 cm) on all sides.

2 Construct the sides of the box using the molding. Build the box with simple butt joints (see illustration below). Use both glue and brads to join the boards.

3 Using the box just constructed, measure and cut the ¼-inch (6 mm) plywood or paneling to fit the box. Attach this piece to the backside of the box using both glue and brads.

4 Paint the box and the frame any way you want. This frame was painted using the crackle technique on page 20.

5 Lay the frame facedown, and center the box on the frame. Place the hinges where you want them, and mark the location for the screws with the awl. Screw the hinges to the frame and box.

6 Position and attach the cabinet magnet set.

7 Locate and drill the hole for the small cabinet knob. It may be necessary to countersink the back of this hole so the

screw and nut don't interfere with closing the "door."

8 The last step of construction is to position the key hooks. Care must be taken to locate these hooks for _your_ keys. Some keys are larger than others and shouldn't drag on the shelf.

9 The method used to hang this box should allow the box to remain flat against the wall and be strong enough to withstand the repeated opening of the box.

10 There are many options for the opening of the frame. You can use the glass that comes with the frame or add a photo or picture to the glass. Hardware cloth or chicken wire looks nice as well.

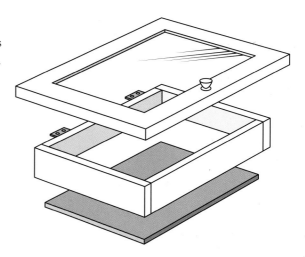

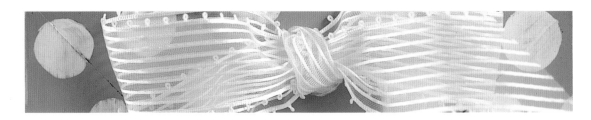

Distressed Dots

DESIGNER: ALLISON SMITH

This slightly distressed frame is a great complement for a birth announcement or a baby's first photograph.

WHAT YOU NEED

Wooden frame, any size

Mint green acrylic paint

Round stencil or something round that's the desired size of the polka dots

White acrylic paint

Small paintbrush

Ruler

Drill with ⅜-inch (1 cm) bit

Fine-grit sandpaper

White sheer organza ribbon

Scissors

WHAT YOU DO

1 Find a green frame or paint the frame with one or two coats of mint green acrylic paint. Let it dry.

2 Use the round stencil or object to trace polka dots randomly over the frame.

3 Paint the polka dots with two coats of the white paint. Let the polka dots dry.

4 Use the ruler to help find the top center of the frame, and mark it with a small pencil dot. Measure out from the center ¾ inch (1.9 cm) on each side, and mark each with a small dot. These outside dots mark where the ribbon will come in from the back, so adjust the measurement according to the size of the frame and your personal preference.

5 Drill holes in the frame at the two outside dots.

6 Distress the frame by sanding it with the sandpaper until you're happy with the look.

7 Thread the organza ribbon through the holes, and tie it in a bow on the front side of the frame. Trim the ends.

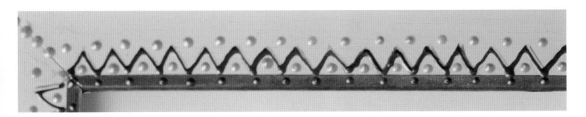

Copper Cross-Stitch

DESIGNER: SUZANNE NICAUD

Create an intricate "cross-stitch" with copper foil tape and craft paint. The lacy open pattern works well on a light-colored frame.

WHAT YOU DO

1 Paint the frame with one or two coats of the cream acrylic spray paint. Let it dry.

2 Estimate the length of copper foil tape needed to completely wrap the outermost corner areas of the frame. Cut the strips.

3 Apply the strips of foil tape carefully to each corner. To avoid crinkling the delicate foil, pull the backing paper away from the foil, rather than pulling the foil away from the backing paper. Burnish small creases flat with the back of your fingernail. Trim away any excess tape on the back side of the frame with the craft knife.

4 Carefully estimate the lengths of foil tape needed to create a fillet (a decorative strip at the inside opening of a frame), and cut the ends of these four strips at a 45° angle.

5 Apply the foil tape to the inside edge of the frame's opening, wrapping it around to the back. Smooth the tape into the corners.

6 Practice applying the paint to a sheet of paper first, to get an idea of how much pressure you'll need to use in order to get an even line and the size of dots that you want. Then, apply a simple zigzag line pattern with the bronze metallic three-dimensional paint, as shown in the photo. Apply dots with the pale gold paint. Let the paint dry thoroughly, according to the manufacturer's directions. The paint is fragile until it's completely dry, so handle the frame with care.

WHAT YOU NEED

Wooden frame, any size

Cream acrylic spray paint

¼-inch (6 mm) adhesive-backed copper foil tape★

Scissors

Craft knife

Three-dimensional craft paint in pale gold and bronze metallic

★Available where stained-glass supplies are sold

Pencil Profusion

DESIGNER: JEAN MOORE

Here's a frame with a lot of class. Play around with assorted designs, and get the family involved so you're not doing all the sharpening yourself.

WHAT YOU NEED

Wooden frame with wide border

Mustard yellow acrylic spray paint

Ruler

5 dozen pencils (plus or minus a few)

Manual pencil sharpener

Electric pencil sharpener (optional)

Hot glue gun and glue sticks

WHAT YOU DO

1 Paint the frame with one or two coats of the mustard yellow spray paint. Let it dry.

2 Measure the outside border of the frame, and sharpen the pencils to fill in the border. (You can use the electric sharpener; however, you'll need the manual one to sharpen pencils down to smaller lengths.) Glue this first row of pencils into place.

3 Plan your pencil placement carefully, and sharpen the pencils accordingly. You can use the project photograph as a guide, or create your own design. Arrange the pencils for a close fit. To create a symmetrical pattern, try to use an even number of pencils sharpened to the same length on adjacent sides of the frame. Face all pencils in the same direction to achieve a uniform look. You may want to wait until you've sharpened and placed all the pencils before gluing them to the frame.

4 Work around the entire frame in this manner, starting at the top and bottom and adjusting the pencil size to fit in on the sides. You can alter the sizes to any length you desire as long as you keep the pencils flowing around the frame.

5 When you come to the center (the last row) sharpen the pencils until they create a neat border around the frame opening.

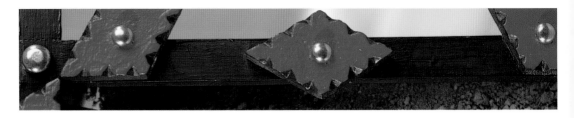

Tramp Art

DESIGNER: TERRY TAYLOR

Tramp art is a wood-working style popularized in the early 1900s, characterized by the notched carving of small pieces of wood for decorating a variety of objects. This example of the art uses basswood diamond shapes attached to a thin wooden frame.

WHAT YOU NEED

Wooden frame with thin borders

Acrylic paints in various colors

Small paintbrushes

Scrap paper

Scissors

¼-inch-thick (6 mm) basswood board (found in hobby and craft stores)

Jigsaw

Sandpaper

Pocketknife

Foam brush

Awl or small, sharp nail

Wood glue

Upholstery tacks

Hammer

WHAT YOU DO

1 Paint the frame with one or two coats of the color of your choice. Let it dry.

2 Draw diamond shapes on paper, and cut them out. The size of the diamonds will depend on the size of your frame. Arrange them on the frame as desired. Sketch the position of the diamonds on the frame for future reference.

3 Transfer the diamond shapes to the basswood, and cut them out with the jigsaw. Sand all edges smooth.

4 Use the pocketknife to make V-cuts on all four edges of each diamond (see photo detail above). To do this, make a shallow, straight cut on an edge about ⅛ inch (3 mm) deep. Angle the knife at either side, and cut toward the first cut. Repeat this on the opposite side of the first cut. A small, wedge-shaped chip should pop out. Move the knife along the edge and make another straight cut. Angle cut again. You should work toward carving evenly spaced and sized cuts. Use a scrap of wood to practice on until you're comfortable with the technique. It really isn't hard to do at all. Carve all of the diamond shapes in this way.

5 Use a very small brush to paint the sides, back, and carved areas of the diamonds with a color to match your frame. Give the shapes additional coats of paint as desired.

6 Sand the top of each diamond lightly. Use the foam brush and a contrasting color of paint to paint the front of the diamond. Use a light touch with the brush, and you'll have very little paint down in the carved portion. If a bit of paint fills the carved area, you can retouch it with a small brush. Let the paint dry.

7 Pierce each diamond in the center with the awl or sharp nail before attaching them to the frame. This will prevent the wood from splitting when you drive in the decorative upholstery tacks. Glue the diamonds to the frame with the wood glue. Clamp or weight the diamonds as desired, and let the glue dry.

Blue Lady

DESIGNER: SUZANNE NICAUD

In this imaginative project, a photographic image isn't contained within the frame—it becomes part of the decorative motif of the frame itself.

WHAT YOU NEED

Wooden frame with oval opening

Ice-blue acrylic craft paint

Paintbrush

Black-and-white laser print or photocopy of image

Scissors

Masking tape

Blender pen★

Spoon

Sheet of white paper

Spray acrylic sealer of your choice

4.5 mm round faceted acrylic jewels, multicolored

7 mm oval faceted acrylic jewels, multicolored

White craft glue

Toothpicks

★See page 95 for information on suppliers.

WHAT YOU DO

1 Paint the frame with one or two coats of the ice-blue acrylic paint. Let it dry.

2 Scan or photocopy your photographic image. Keep in mind that the photo transfer process will reverse the image, so, if necessary, scan or copy the image in "mirror-image" mode. For the best results, make a fresh print or photocopy just a few days before doing the transfer process. In the example shown, the figure was scanned with image software, then isolated from its background, before being printed on a laser printer. This software is available on rental computers at some copy centers.

3 To eliminate most of the empty white paper around it, cut closely around the figure. This will help you more accurately position the copy onto the frame.

4 Use masking tape to lightly tack the cutout image to the front (and sides, if needed) of the frame.

5 Cover the image area with the blender pen's tip. Try to confine the solvent to the image itself, because it can easily damage the frame's painted surface. The paper should very quickly become nearly transparent, as the toner is transferred to the paper.

6 Remove the masking tape, and carefully peel away the paper. It will stick somewhat to the painted surface, but pull anyway. Burnish any bubbled areas with the back of a spoon and a clean sheet of white paper; they'll flatten right out.

7 Lightly spray the frame with a coat of the acrylic spray sealer, then let it dry.

8 Separate the white, pink, and light blue acrylic jewels from the other colors. Prearrange all of the jewels into position around the perimeter of the oval opening.

9 Pick up your first jewel. Use a toothpick to apply a small dot of craft glue to the back, then put it back into position. Repeat with all of the jewels.

10 Apply a pair of oval jewels at the corner of each side of the frame.

Luxurious Leather

DESIGNER: ALLISON SMITH

A scrap of leather and a handful of upholstery tacks will transform any plain old frame into a handsome accessory befitting the most elegant decor.

WHAT YOU NEED

Wooden frame, any size

Scrap of leather bigger than the frame

Hot glue gun and glue sticks or spray adhesive

Craft knife

Scissors

Upholstery tacks

Hammer

WHAT YOU DO

1 Place the leather on a flat surface, right-side down.

2 Cover the front of the frame with a thin coat of hot glue. Immediately place it in the center of the leather. Turn the frame over and smooth the leather out.

3 Place the frame facedown on the work surface. Using the craft knife, cut out from the outside corners at a 90° angle, thus creating four notched corners.

4 Run a thin line of glue down one side of the frame. Fold the leather over to secure it to the frame. Press to adhere. Standing the frame on its edge, trim the excess leather away with the craft knife. Repeat with the remaining edges.

5 Make a small slit in the center of the leather, and make a large X all the way to the inside corners. This part can be tricky; make sure to cut into the corners far enough so the leather doesn't pucker when you glue it down, but not so much that the cut is visible. Fold the inside edge pieces over the inside of the frame, and secure with glue. Trim away excess leather.

6 Place the frame faceup on the work surface. Hammer the upholstery tacks onto the front of the frame in any desired pattern.

Fabric Fantasia
DESIGNER: SUZANNE NICAUD

Since this project uses less than ¼ yard (.23 m) of fabric, you can splurge on a really fancy piece. Choose a fabric that coordinates with your decorating scheme. The hand-dyed and embroidered silk fabric used on this frame was found in a shop that specializes in imports.

WHAT YOU DO

1 Measure the length and width of the frame. Cut one piece of the batting for each of the four sides of the frame. Lay the end of one of the shorter pieces on top of one of the longer ones, and stitch them together at a 45° angle; trim away the excess at the corner, as shown in figure 1 on page 72. Join all the pieces together in this way, until you have a "frame" of the batting material.

2 Hot glue the "frame" of batting material to the front of the frame.

3 Measure the length of one of the 45° angles plus twice the depth of the frame. The length and width of the fabric pieces must be equal to the front outer measurements of the frame plus enough extra to be able to wrap around the inside edges, the outside edges, and a bit of the back.

4 With their right sides together, baste one long and one short piece of fabric together at a 45° angle. Start a short distance from the edge of the fabric, and baste only the length of the mitered corner-plus-frame-depth, so that later you can neatly wrap the fabric at the inner and outer corners (see figure 2).

WHAT YOU NEED

Wooden frame, any size

Ruler

Polyester quilt batting

Scissors

Thread in a complementary color

Needle or sewing machine

Hot glue gun and glue sticks

Lightweight fabric

Putty knife (optional)

5 Baste the next piece onto the fabric as you did in step 3, checking carefully that the seams fall at the mitered corners of the frame. For the best fit, continue adding the pieces one at a time. When the fabric pieces are all correctly positioned to make the fabric cover, with a small amount of fabric overlapping the frame's opening and a larger amount overlapping at the outer edges, stitch the seams. Clip off the corners, trim the excess fabric, and press the seam allowances open.

6 Lay the fabric frame facedown onto your work surface, then position the wood frame facedown on top of the fabric. Apply hot glue to an inner corner of the frame, then adhere the fabric smoothly to it. If your fabric is very sheer, use a putty knife to press it onto the hot glue. Repeat the gluing for the opposite corner, then glue the other two corners.

7 Glue the inside edges for all four sides of the frame's opening. Do these neatly, pressing the fabric flat into the glue; otherwise your glass, mat, picture, and backing board may not fit back into the recess. As long as the glue is warm, you'll find you can reposition the fabric slightly, if necessary. Check the position of the fabric over the frame's face.

8 Beginning with one of the short sides, apply hot glue along the side. Adhere the fabric smoothly, neatly folding in the fabric at the corners and applying more glue as needed to pull the fabric around to the back of the frame. Continue wrapping the rest of the frame; in order for the fabric's tension to be equal, work on opposing sides.

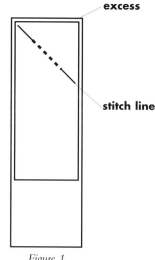

Figure 1

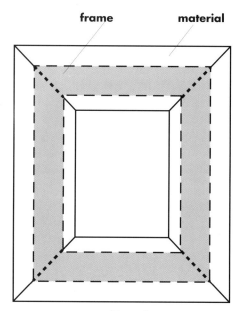

Figure 2

Dice-y Design

DESIGNER: MARTHE LE VAN

Don't worry if you don't have a whole bunch of dice around. You can go to hobby stores and pick up a bag for a reasonable price. And if dice don't do it for you, try dominoes or mah-jongg game pieces.

WHAT YOU DO

1 Use a black frame, or paint the frame with one or more coats of black acrylic spray paint. Let it dry.

2 Start randomly attaching dice to the frame with the hot glue. Vary the angles of the dice, the numbers of the dice, and their spacing according to your own desires. You can even get crazy and let a few dice hang off the interior and exterior edges of the frame.

3 If you're not the gambling sort, you can always place all the dice on the frame before gluing them on, and play with the design until you're happy with it.

WHAT YOU NEED

Wooden frame

Black acrylic spray paint

Hot glue gun and glue sticks

Lots of dice

Metallic Leaves

DESIGNER: ALLISON SMITH

Use either fresh or dried leaves (smaller leaves work best) to produce this wonderful frame that creates the illusion of glittering, sun-reflected leaves scattering about on a windswept autumn afternoon.

WHAT YOU NEED

Wooden frame, any size

Black acrylic spray paint

20 to 25 pressed Japanese maple leaves (or leaves of your choice)

Newspaper

Spray foil leaf adhesive

Decoupage medium (optional)

Simulated gold and silver foil leaf

Small paintbrush

Paper towels or soft cloth

Spray mount

Clear spray acrylic sealer

Gold paste

WHAT YOU DO

1 Use a black frame, or paint a frame with one or two coats of black acrylic spray paint. Let it dry.

2 Lay the maple leaves faceup on a sheet of newspaper. Spray them with the foil leaf adhesive. If the leaves are too dry, they'll break when they're attached to the frame. In that case, use decoupage medium thinned with a little water instead of spray adhesive to attach the leaves to the frame.

3 Take one leaf at a time, and place it onto a piece of foil leaf. Use the small, dry paintbrush to help secure the foil onto the maple leaf.

4 Rub the paper towel or soft cloth over the surface of the leaves. This burnishes the simulated leaf and gives it a nice sheen while also removing any excess leaf.

5 Place the leaves foil-side down on a piece of newspaper. Spray them with the spray mount.

6 Arrange the leaves, and press them around the edges of the frame, alternating gold and silver leaves as you go.

7 Spray the entire frame with several coats of the acrylic sealer.

8 Use your index finger to create a swirling vein of gold around the border of the frame with the gold paste.

Partly Cloudy
DESIGNER: DIANA LIGHT

Grab some paint and sponges, and get lost in the clouds with this wistful, day-dreamy frame.

WHAT YOU DO

1 Paint the frame with the sky-blue acrylic paint. Let it dry.

2 Place the enlarged template (see page 94) on the frame, and trace the outlines of the clouds and stars with a pencil so that a slight impression is left on the frame. Continue the cloud shapes onto the outside and inside edges of the frame. Use these lines as a guide to paint in.

3 Mix the white paint with some silver in the muffin-style palette. Thoroughly wet the sponge, then squeeze it very dry. If it's new, squeeze mild sudsy water through it first, then rinse it before starting.

4 Get paint on the sponge, and press the sponge onto the wax paper repeatedly until you get the amount of paint/texture you like.

5 Sponge the bottom parts of the clouds; it's okay to let it overlap into the rest of the clouds a little. Let it dry.

6 Use just white paint to sponge in the rest of the clouds. Let a little bit of the paint overlap outside the lines along one side of each cloud. Let it dry.

7 Use the liner brush and silver paint to outline the cloud shapes (going over the line impression you made at the beginning).

8 Use the liner brush and yellow paint, and fill in the stars. Let it dry.

9 Spray the frame lightly with one or two coats of the sealer.

WHAT YOU NEED

Wooden frame, any size

Acrylic paints in sky blue, white, silver, and yellow

Paintbrush

Template (see page 94)

Muffin tin-style plastic paint palette

Sponge (beauty wedge, kitchen, or natural sea)

Wax paper

Fine, round brush (liner brush)

Spray acrylic sealer of your choice

Beach Memories

DESIGNER: SUSAN RIND

After that memorable vacation to the beach, empty your pockets and create this memento frame (with or without the fun dragonfly).

WHAT YOU NEED

Wooden frame, any size

Acrylic spray paint, your choice of color (optional)

20-gauge silver-plate wire, 30 inches long (76.2 cm)

Wire cutters

Needle-nose pliers

Approximately 10 assorted crystal beads, 4 mm to 12 mm in size

2-½-inch (6.4 cm) cylindrical bead

12 mm round bead

Jewelry glue or epoxy

Assorted beach collectibles, including driftwood, rocks, shells, and glass

Toothpicks

WHAT YOU DO

1 Paint the frame, if necessary. To make the dragonfly, first bend the silver-plate wire in half. With the pliers, twist two times at the bend, creating a small loop.

2 Next, feed in three crystal beads for the tail. Add the cylindrical bead for the body.

3 With the two wire ends coming out of the cylindrical bead, make four wings approximately 1 inch (2.5 cm) long each. Twist them together in the center.

4 Feed the two wire ends through the 12 mm round bead.

5 On each wire end, add two crystal beads for antennae.

6 Bend the remaining wire ends down to the center of the dragonfly's body, twist, and add three 8 mm beads to cover the twist.

7 Finish the dragonfly by looping the wire over an oval bead, and place the finishing ends underneath the dragonfly's body. Place the dragonfly aside.

8 Use a toothpick to apply the glue to the beach collectibles. Glue pieces on the frame so the presentation is balanced. Let the glue dry. Glue the dragonfly where you want it.

Lazy Mosaic

DESIGNER: TERRY TAYLOR

If mosaics appeal to you, but mixing grout is not your idea of a good time, then this is the mosaic project for you. Not much fuss and no muss.

WHAT YOU NEED

Wooden frame, any size

Acrylic spray paint, your choice of color

Pre-tumbled stones, tiles, china shards, or glass

Rock tumbler (optional)

Jewelry glue or epoxy

WHAT YOU DO

1 You can purchase a wide variety of pre-tumbled materials in craft or bead stores. If you have access to a hobbyist's rock tumbler, you can tumble your own material. Follow the manufacturer's instructions for using a tumbler. It won't take much more than a day to tumble china, tiles, or glass for a sea-worn appearance.

2 Spray the frame with a couple of coats of acrylic paint. Select a color that will complement or contrast with the tumbled materials you've chosen.

3 Lay the frame on a flat surface. Lay the tumbled material on the frame. Play with the placement of the pieces until you're satisfied with the effect. You may want to try placing some of your materials so they hang over the opening or over the edges of the frame.

4 Use the jewelry glue or epoxy to attach the materials to the frame. Let the glue dry according to the manufacturer's recommendations. You can also use hot glue if you want.

This playful frame is decorated with randomly scattered drilled holes and tiny, painted polka dots. Home improvement stores carry assorted drill bits at reasonable prices.

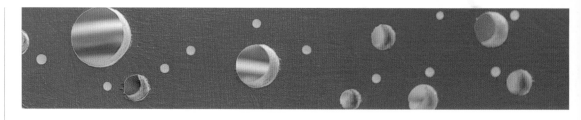

Hole-ly Moly
DESIGNER: TERRY TAYLOR

WHAT YOU DO

1 Drill a few holes with the largest size drill bit you have. Be careful not to place holes where they might interfere with the frame opening. Then, change drill bits and drill more holes, spacing them as desired. When drilling, always place a piece of scrap wood under the frame. It will lessen the likelihood of your frame splitting on the back where the drill exits, not to mention preventing accidental holes in your dining room table or living room floor.

2 Use the sandpaper to smooth any rough edges. Roll up the sandpaper in a tube shape to sand the insides of the holes.

3 Once you're happy with the number of holes, give the frame a coat of primer. Let it dry. Sand the frame lightly. Pay particular attention to the insides of the holes. A second coat of primer is recommended.

4 Use a small brush to paint the insides of the holes. Don't worry about getting paint on the face or back of the frame. You can sand it off later. Let the paint dry. Paint the holes with additional coats as desired.

5 Sand the frame lightly. Remove any excess paint near the edges of the holes.

6 Paint the face and back of the frame. Use a deft touch near the edges of the holes. Let the first coat dry. Give the frame additional coats of paint as needed.

7 Add very tiny dots to the frame to fool the eye. Use the handle end of a small brush to make dots. Simply dip the tip of the handle in a bit of paint, and stamp it on the frame. Add dots as desired. Let the paint dry.

8 Spray the frame lightly with one or two coats of the sealer.

WHAT YOU NEED

Wooden frame, any size

Drill, with assorted bits

Scrap of wood

Sandpaper, in a variety of grits

Acrylic primer

Paintbrush

Small paintbrush

Acrylic paint in magenta and tangerine

Spray acrylic sealer of your choice

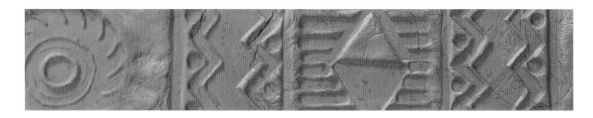

Clay Play

DESIGNER: LINDA RAGSDALE

Get your hands dirty with this easy, no-bake clay frame. Your design choices are unlimited, and if you don't wish to use rubber stamps, you can create a faux mosaic or inlaid glass look with dimensional glass paint.

WHAT YOU NEED

Picture frame, any size

3 or 4 sheets of paper

Decorative rubber stamps of your choice

Air-dry terra cotta clay

Plastic bead with raised decorative pattern

Varnish or sealer (optional)

WHAT YOU DO

1 Trace the frame onto the sheets of paper, and play around with the stamps until you create a pattern you like.

2 With your fingers, cover the frame with clay, about ¼ inch (6 mm) thick. Don't forget to cover the inside and outside edges. For a smoother finish, dip your fingers in water to smooth out the clay as you cover the frame.

3 If you smoothed the clay with water, wait until the surface is no longer slick before stamping. Stamping into wet clay may lift the clay off the frame. Press the rubber stamps into the soft clay, following the design you came up with in step 1. If you make a mistake, or you don't like the design after all, smooth the clay out and start over.

4 Roll the bead around the perimeter of the photo window.

5 Let the clay air dry, and celebrate the natural cracks that occur. If a smooth finish is desired, watch for cracks during the drying process, and use water to smooth them out.

6 Seal the frame with a spray or brush-on sealer, but be patient. Due to the porous nature of clay, you may need to spray several times before you get a consistent coat.

Give an ordinary frame a majestic makeover with some pink fur, ribbons, faux flowers, glitter, pieces of garland, and anything else you can find that would please the little princess in your life.

Princess Power

DESIGNER: DIANA LIGHT

WHAT YOU NEED

Beveled wooden frame★

Pink faux fur

Scissors

Hot glue gun and glue sticks

Piece of garland or corsage (or other found "princessy" items)

Posterboard or card board (optional)

Pink ribbon

Faux flowers, netting, glitter, etc.

Small faux flowers

★The beveled frame enhances the curve of the "garland," but this project also works well with a flat frame.

WHAT YOU DO

1 Place the faux fur on your work sur-face with the fur side facedown. Place the frame on top of the fur, and adhere the fur to one outside edge of the frame with the hot glue.

2 Cut out the rectangle for the opening in the middle of the fur, leaving plenty of fur to cover all the inside edges of the frame's opening.

3 Glue the fur to the inside edge of the same side of the frame in which you glued the outside edge in step 1.

4 Glue the fur to the rest of the inside edges.

5 Cut and glue the rest of the outside edges. The fur should now completely cover the frame. Snip away any extra fur from the glued sides.

6 Trim the top of the frame with a piece of garland or corsage. To make your own, cut a ¼-inch-wide (6 mm) strip of posterboard or cardboard just slightly shorter than the width of the frame. Wrap and glue the ribbon around it. Then attach artificial flowers, netting, glitter, ribbons, etc., to the trim with the hot glue.

7 Attach the piece just below the top edge of the frame with the hot glue.

8 Glue little cloth flowers to the ends of the pink ribbons.

9 Cut the ribbons to different lengths, some longer than the frame. Glue the ribbons to the decorative piece at the top corners. Glue a flower over each top cor-ner. When displaying on a tabletop, arrange the ribbons on the table in front of the frame. Your majesty awaits!

Message Board

DESIGNER: LINDA RAGSDALE

Corkboards are useful, but they're also dreadfully boring. So, decorate your office, kitchen, or wherever you keep your phone with a message center that has an interesting center.

WHAT YOU NEED

Picture frame, any size

Roll of thin cork material

Scissors

Ruler

Craft glue

Thin plastic scraper

Craft knife

Rub-on transfers

Spray acrylic sealer of your choice

WHAT YOU DO

1 Place the frame onto an unrolled section of corkboard, and cut off an ample amount of cork to cover the surface and edges of the frame. Measure the exact widths of the frame edges, and cut strips of cork to cover all four sides of the frame, and all four of the inner edges.

2 With the scraper, smooth an even layer of glue over the edges of the frame, and attach the strips. Smooth another layer of glue over the top surface of the frame, making sure not to let the glue overrun the edges. Cover the top of the surface with the cork. Let the glue set.

3 From the back side of the frame, trim away excess cork where the edge strips meet the top cork cover. Carefully cut out the picture window.

4 Cut out individual rub-on transfer shapes and place the shapes in the areas you wish to apply them. When you have finalized your design, follow the manufacturer's instructions and apply the transfers. Make sure you apply enough pressure to adhere them to the uneven surface of the cork.

5 Spray the frame with one or two coats of the sealer.

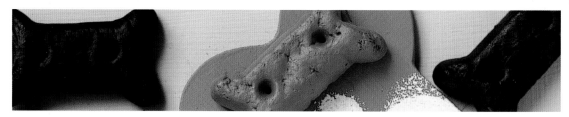

Embellish your favorite photograph of your four-legged friend with this over-the-top bone-anza of a frame.

Doggy Treat

DESIGNER: MARTHE LE VAN

WHAT YOU NEED

Wooden frame, any size

Acrylic craft paints in light blue, medium blue, dark blue, green, and white

Paintbrush

Sponge paintbrush

Fine-tip paintbrush

Small dog bones

4 prefabricated wooden dog bones

Fine-grit sandpaper

2 round sponge stencil brushes, ½ inch (1.3 cm) and ¼ inch (6 mm) in diameter

Plastic lid

Hot glue gun and glue sticks

Wooden chopstick or craft stick

WHAT YOU DO

1 Paint the frame with one or two coats of the light blue acrylic craft paint. Let it dry.

2 Select dog bones to use on the frame. Using the sponge paintbrush and the medium blue acrylic craft paint, cover the front side and all visible edges of half of the real dog bones. (The fine-tip paintbrush may come in handy for reaching small areas.) Let the bones dry.

3 Using the sponge paintbrush and the dark blue acrylic craft paint, cover the front side and all visible edges of the rest of the dog bones. Let them dry.

4 Smooth the edges of the four wooden dog bones with the fine-grit sandpaper. Remove all dust from the bones with a damp rag.

5 Use the sponge paintbrush to paint the wooden dog bones with the green acrylic craft paint.

6 Pour a small amount of the white acrylic craft paint onto the plastic lid. Press the larger sponge stencil brush into the paint, then test-stamp it onto a scrap of colored paper until you're satisfied with the results. This will be the large paw pad print.

7 Stamp one white circle onto the center bottom edge of each of the painted wooden dog bones. Switch to the smaller sponge stencil paintbrush, and using the same technique, create four paw pad prints above the large pad print.

8 Arrange the painted bones on the frame to form the design you want. (You can use the project photograph as your guide, or make up a pattern all your own. Leaving some bones off, and painting your dog's name on the frame would be a great variation!)

9 Evenly spread hot glue onto the back of one real dog bone, and press the bone onto the wooden dog bone. Firmly hold the bone in place until the glue bonds with the wood. Following your design, affix the rest of the dog bones to the wooden bones.

10 Glue both the real and wooden dog bones to the frame.

Stamp Play

DESIGNER: TERRY TAYLOR

Flat-faced frames are perfect surfaces for rubber stamping. Whether you use a purchased stamp or carve your own (it's easy to do), you'll be pleased with the sophisticated results.

WHAT YOU NEED

Flat wooden frame, any size

Acrylic paint of your choice

Paintbrush

Newsprint or white paper

Rubber stamp

Rubber stamp ink

Clear acetate

Craft knife

White acrylic paint

Stencil brush

WHAT YOU DO

1 Paint the frame with several coats of the acrylic paint.

2 Place the frame on a sheet of newsprint. Trace around the frame's dimensions. Use this traced image to plan the pattern you'll create with your rubber stamps. Ink your stamp and stamp it on the tracing as desired. If you don't like the pattern you're creating, make another tracing and try as many design patterns as you wish. It's easier to plan the design ahead of time rather than proceeding directly to the frame.

3 Create a stencil (in this case a rectangle sized to fit the stamp used in this project) by tracing a shape onto clear acetate. Cut it out with the craft knife.

4 Mix a small amount of white paint with your acrylic paint. Load the stencil brush with paint, and pounce it on newsprint until it's almost dry.

5 Position the stencil shape on the frame, and apply a light coat of paint. Load the brush and pounce it as needed to achieve the depth of color you wish to achieve. Let the shape dry. Create as many shapes around the frame as your design dictates.

6 Ink your rubber stamp, and stamp it on the frame as desired.

Templates

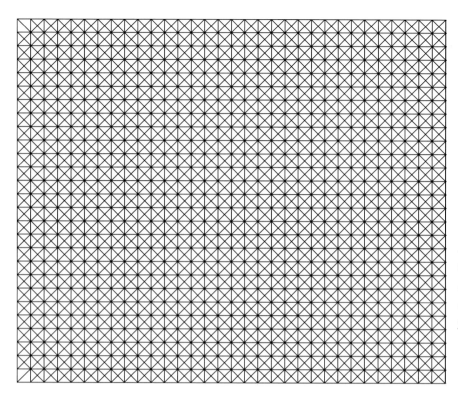

Enlarge this template for Faux Metallic on page 22 to fit your frame.

Enlarge this template for Architect's Dream on page 30 to fit your frame.

Enlarge this template for Partly Cloudy on page 76 to fit your frame.

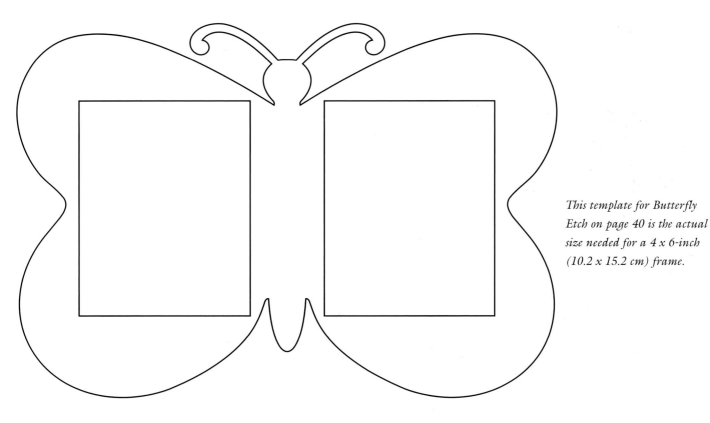

This template for Butterfly Etch on page 40 is the actual size needed for a 4 x 6-inch (10.2 x 15.2 cm) frame.

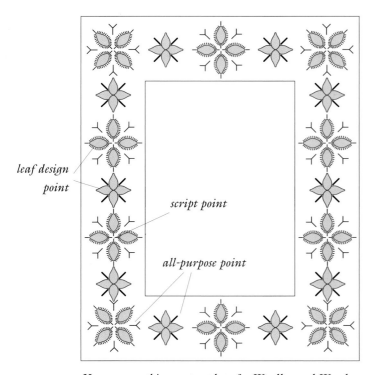

leaf design point

script point

all-purpose point

You can use this as a template for Woodburned Wonder on page 52, or simply refer to it when deciding which points to use for the design elements.

A NOTE ABOUT SUPPLIERS

Usually, the supplies you need for making the projects in Lark books can be found at your local craft supply store, discount mart, home improvement center, or retail shop relevant to the topic of the book. Occasionally, however, you may need to buy materials or tools from specialty suppliers. In order to provide you with the most up-to-date information, we have created a listing of suppliers on our web site, which we update on a regular basis. Visit us at www.larkbooks.com, click on "Craft Supply Sources," and then click on the relevant topic. You will find numerous companies listed with their web address and/or mailing address and phone number.

DESIGNER BIOGRAPHIES

DALE AND PAULA HEYES live in Asheville, North Carolina, and enjoy working together, designing and making things for their home and family.

SUSAN KIEFFER enjoys dabbling in a variety of crafts, from designing fountains, to decorating candles and baskets, to creating mosaic-tile countertops. She is assistant editor of FiberArts Magazine, the magazine of textiles, published in Asheville, North Carolina.

Some kids mow the grass or do the dishes to earn their allowance. Not MARTHE LE VAN. Her painter-mom introduced her to the joys of framing at an early age. She garnered pocket money assembling metal frames and, much to the chagrin of her young tender fingertips, attaching hanging wires. This innocent task proved pivotal in Marthe's professional pursuits as a curator, exhibition manager, and craft designer.

DIANA LIGHT lives and works in the beautiful Blue Ridge Mountains of North Carolina. Her home studio, like her life, is surrounded by glittering glass in hundreds of forms, styles, and types. After earning her B.F.A. in painting and print-making, she extended her expertise to etching and painting fine glass objects. She has contributed to numerous Lark books and is the coauthor of Lark's *The Weekend Crafter: Etching Glass*.

JEAN TOMASO MOORE is a part-time multimedia artist who has been creating art in one form or another for as long as she can remember. She lives with her humble and patient husband in Asheville, North Carolina.

SUZANNE NICAUD was born in Limoges, France. Trained as a seamstress, she relocated to the States in 1955, and now lives in Indiana. Her daughter, Suzanne, often uses this name as a pseudonym.

LINDA RAGSDALE is a craftsman whose joy lies in demonstrating alternative purposes for common items or using odd items to craft with. Her goal is to help people open their creative gates to further develop their own sense of art. She works with her sister at a company called Mixed Nuts, where they manufacture recycled triple-thick cardboard, perfect for any crafting medium, into frames, home accents and even furniture. Her cardboard crafts can be viewed in the Lark publication, *Creative Cardboard: Making Fabulous Furniture, Amazing Accessories and Other Spectacular Stuff.*

SUSAN RIND is the designer for Dustin Designs. She takes her inspiration from nature to create her chic home decor and fashion accessories line. She shows her work twice a year at the Pacific Designer Collection in New York City, and her work is retailed in gift galleries and exclusive clothing stores throughout the United States and Canada.

ALLISON SMITH lives in Asheville, North Carolina. Her home-based business specializes in providing deluxe tourist accommodations in remote locations in Western North Carolina. She is an avid crafter and designer in addition to being a full-time mother. She has created projects for numerous Lark books including *Decorating Baskets*, *Girls' World*, and *Decorating Candles*.

TERRY TAYLOR is a mixed media artist whose work has been shown in numerous exhibitions. He is a full-time employee of Lark Books.

ACKNOWLEDGMENTS

I would like to thank Robert Todd, Susan and Allen Roderick, and Dana Irwin for letting us take over their homes in search of the perfect locations to photograph the frames in this book. A special thanks is due to Sandra Stambaugh, Dana Irwin, and Hannes Charen for putting together such a lovely book. Another special thanks is owed to the other "authors" of this book: all the terribly talented designers who contributed projects. Also thanks to everyone who contributed artwork and photographs for the frames, especially Sandra Stambaugh. Finally, thank you Paige Gilchrist for your friendship and support.